The Condemnable Mathew Arnold

Written: 1994

Dover Beach is contaminated with the waste of careless others

Hypodermics wash upon the shore of what was once Dover Beach

55 gallon drums float amongst dead gulls in murky crude oil upon the stormy waters of Dover Beach

I walked through the purple sands among the dried carcasses of the fish who washed ashore last night

Victims of the fallout, looking for you.

You were not to be found.

I watched a whale beach himself, tired of trying to swim in the flow of the water that now crashed around him on the shores of Dover Beach.

I thought, 'maybe he was looking for you too,' or maybe he'd found you at Dover Beach.

The sky grew Dark and the acid rain began to fall while the water crashed harder on the shores of Dover Beach, but you were still nowhere to be found.

Maybe you were taking comfort in the shelter of another while I stood in the rain and melted. . . .waiting and looking where I thought I'd find you.

Where I thought I'd brought you.

Where I thought I'd left you.

Where I thought I'd put you

Where I finally found myself alone.

On the shores of Dover Beach.

The beached whale gasped one last dying breath, on the shores of Dover Beach, saying "correct me if I'm wrong, but this looks like New Jersey."

That's when I wept as I melted into the sands of Dover Beach

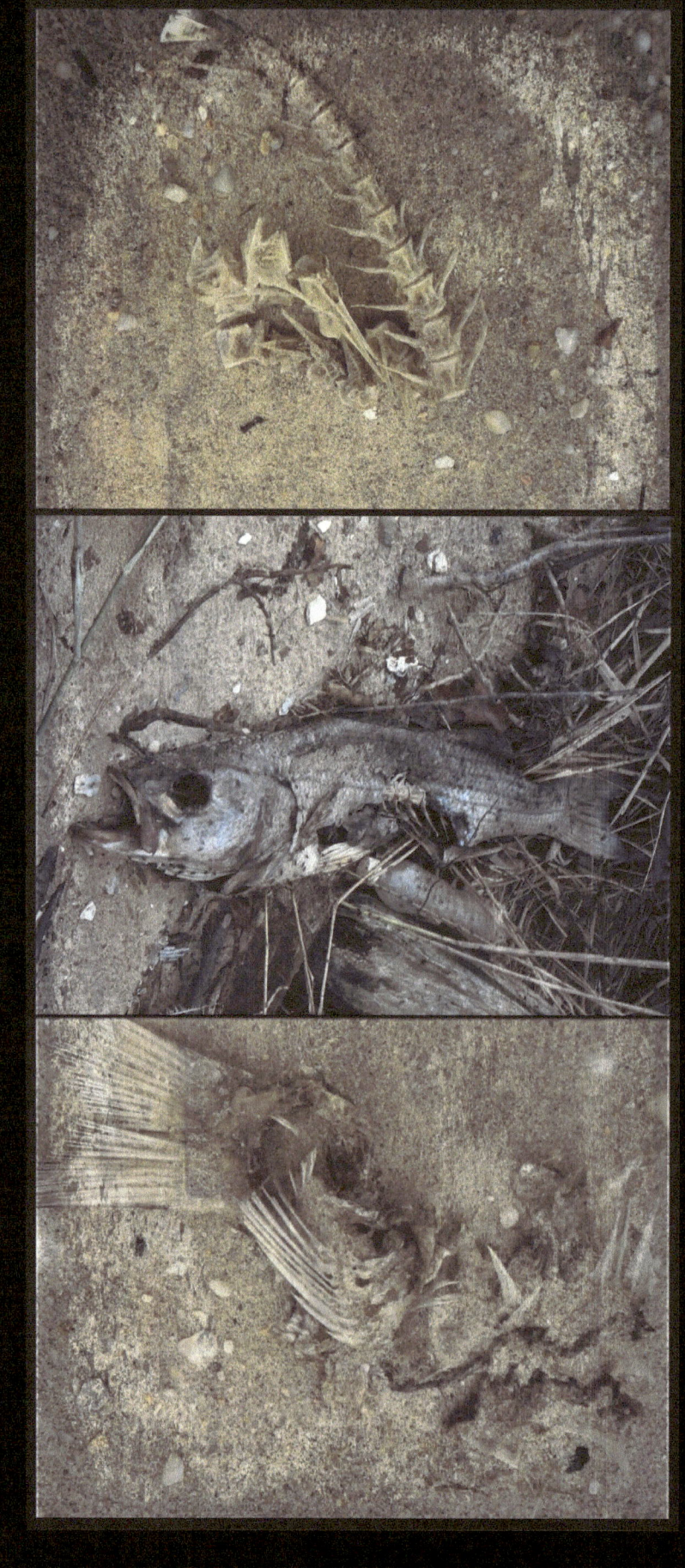

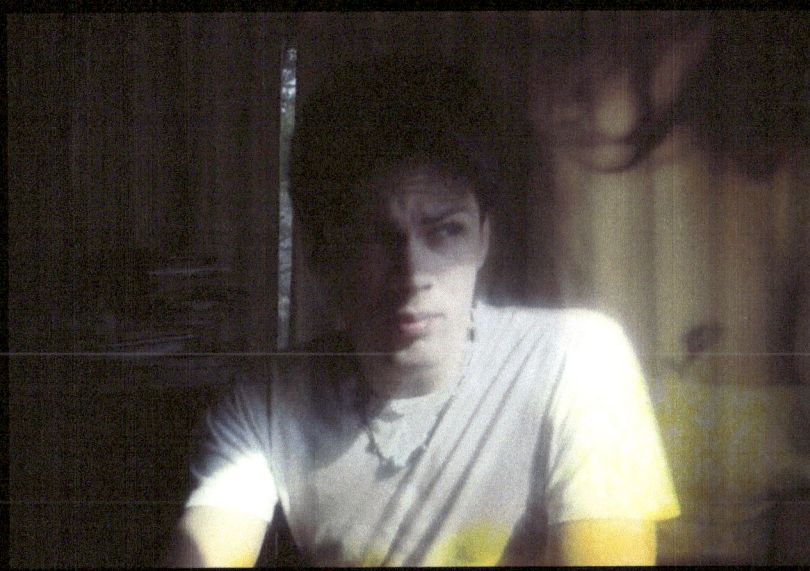

The little match girl

Once I had a match

I would hold it in my hands forever and just stare at it.

One day I lit the match

The spark turned to flame reflecting all the colors of the rainbow: blue, green, red , purple

The flames danced for a moment, then stabilized . the light it emitted shown like a thousand stars and could be seen from far away.

The heat that radiated warmed every ounce of my being.

It warmed me to my very soul.

I couldn't take my eyes off of the glow. The fires unleashed feelings from within me I had never known.

I never thought that such feelings existed within me.

Then, without warning, it burned me.

The searing, the stinging, sharp, pain forced me to release the match.

It fell to the floor . . . . extinguished.

It left me in the cold darkness with only the smell of the smoke and the burns upon my hands that were left to remind me of the grandeur I once felt.

I'm not sure if I'll ever light another, or even if I even feel the urge.

Maybe I should have gotten a lighter.

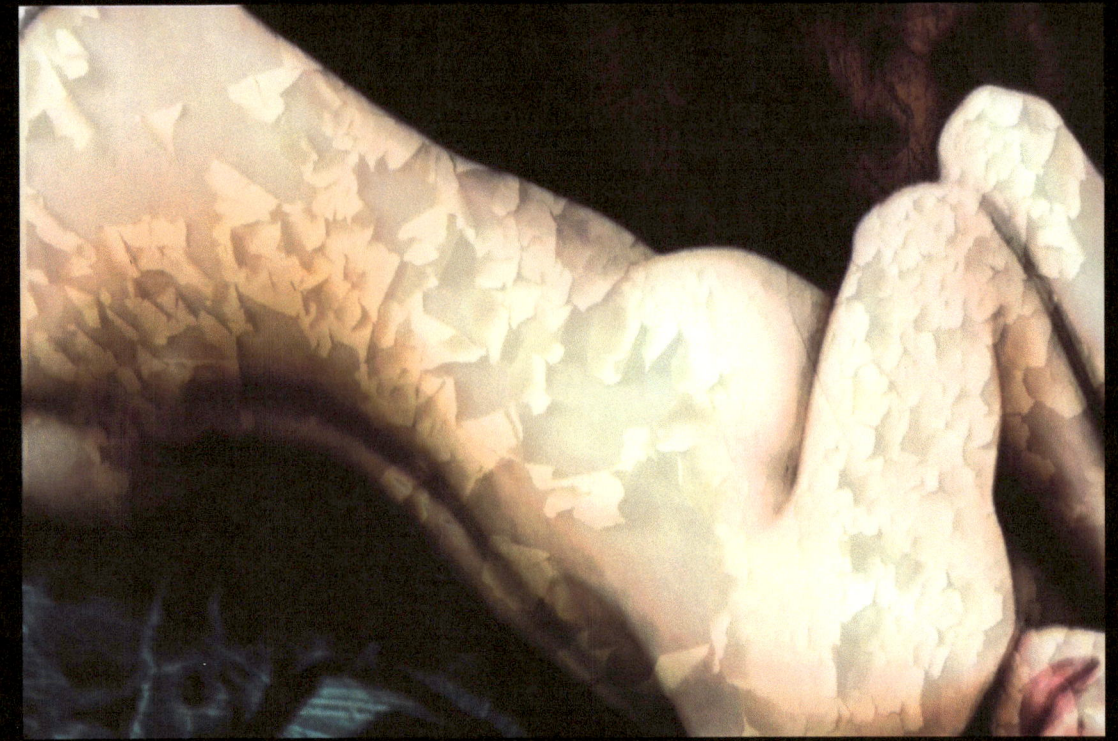

The Whore

Written: 10/29/95

When she gazed at me with her piercing green eyes; that struck the very core of my meager existence, as she slowly pulled the mirrored "Lennon" framed sunglasses that seemed to reflect the world as it should be seen by all through her eyes from her slightly ill proportioned nose . . . .

I knew she was offering me the only thing she knew how to administer to help soothe the pain felt from deep within my damaged soul. Even though I knew neither the gift nor the sympathy would help fill the emptiness felt inside of me . . . . . .

I accepted anyway.

For a few hours I would not be alone. No time for thoughts of sorrow, sadness, death.

Tomorrow it will all be the same, it will all start again.

 if she gets too close, she will eventually pushed away by the man with no passions, no feelings, who longs for the day when her love can be accepted and returned.

For now she is, in his eyes, an instrument, a tool, a whore.

She cannot offer me salvation.

That's Life

Written: 1996

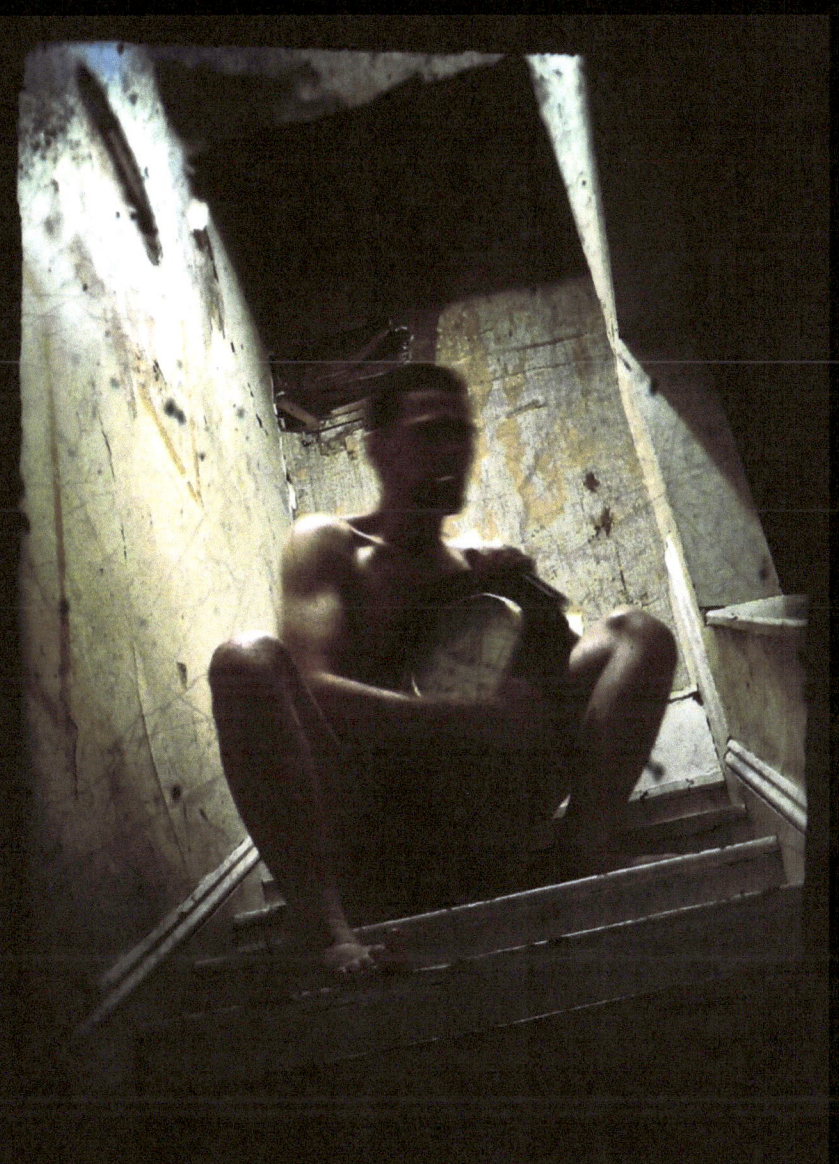

So you say I'm high again

And that is the only reason we are friends

And I say that's right

That's life

And it aint right, how you cause me strife

This woman was my wife

This family was my life

That decision can't be right

And I just wanna die

That's life

Now there's no reality

Or at the least it's too perverse for me

I'm not blind as you can see

I'm not trying to make you happy

I'm just trying to be free

That's life

So you say I'm high again

And you don't even want to be friends

I said I'd "love you 'till the end'

That's life

That's life

Inebriated part 1

I don't care where I'm going to now

I just want to get away somehow

But I feel I've got to stand up now

I stand up . . . . . but too tall

I feel like I'm falling to the ground

I need to hold on to the wall

Call me an artist, call me misunderstood

Call me a thief , call me robinhood

I don't care where I am right now

I just want to turn and run back somehow

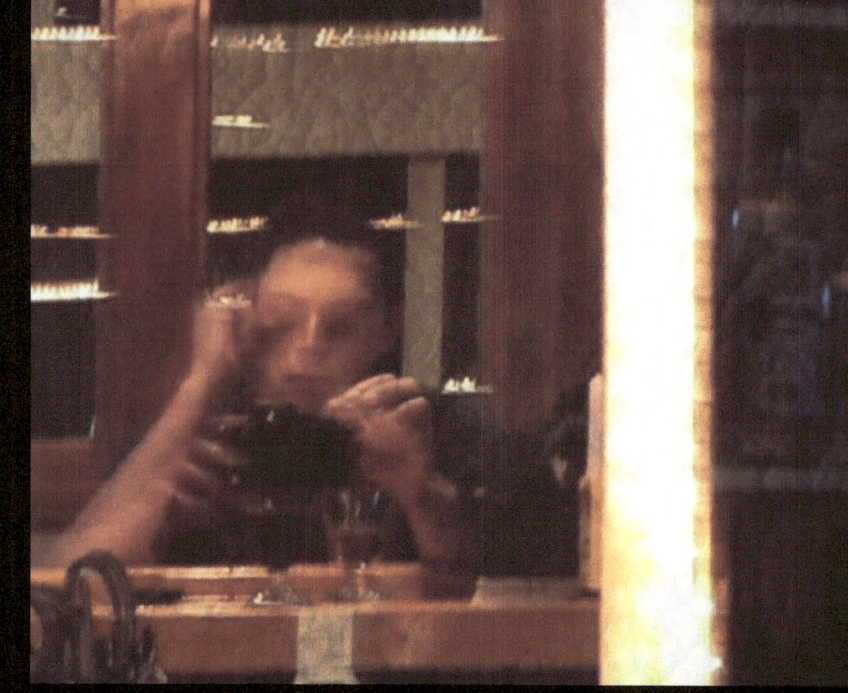

But I feel there's no use to stand up now

I just keep falling down anyhow. I stand up, then I take a fall.

Seems like I drag you all down . . . . I need to hold on to the wall

Call me a poet, call me a pig

Call me nothing, call me big

I don't know where you are now, I wanna say I'm sorry but I don't know how.

But there's no use to stand up now

What goes up, must come down . . . . my head keeps spinning round

what you need to find

There are times when hope finds
you

I've stared death in the eye

In the end I died anyway

Looking for reasons to be hopeful
can leave you hopeless

But it goes on . . . . and on . . . .
. .and on

Half full, half empty, no difference

It still goes on, within, without you

Before you, behind you

At the end of the day, you must

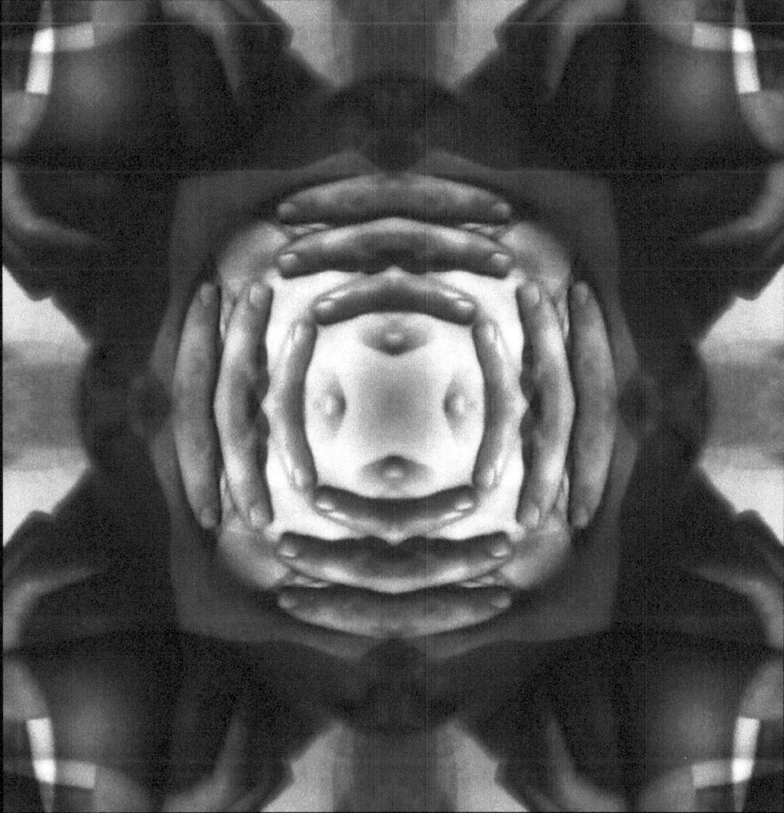

What goes up must come down

My head keeps on spinning round and round

I need to hold onto the wall

Afraid I'm going to take a fall

Call me a coward

Call me a man

Call me callus an in-humane

Call me a beggar

Who comes in a can

I am the melancholy man

I stand up but not too tall

I beat my fist against the wall.

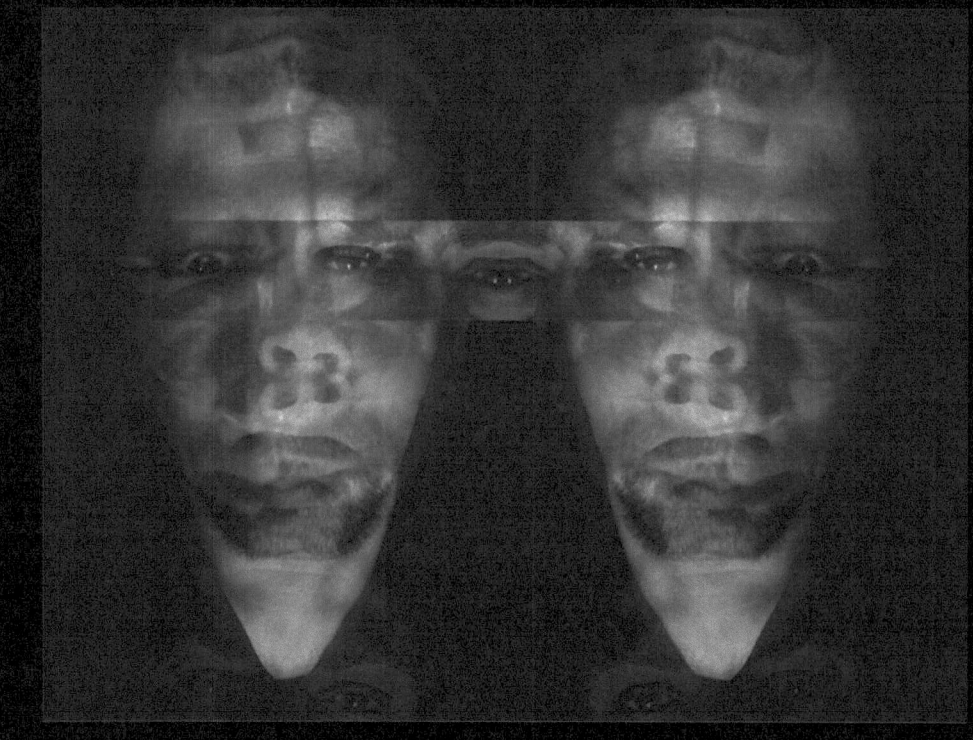

Masters of iniquity part one

Written: 2004

There we stood on the outer edge of hypocrisy looking within from without, seeing all persons scurrying about.

Their destinies planned, their futures were certain, with the wool pulled over their eyes like a curtain.

The conglomerates, the technocracy, the power elite, they played puppeteer while everyone else was asleep.

How could they be so blind? With blank stares on their faces and mass consumption on their mind.

What more can I have? How can I make yours mine? How can I better screw my friends and rob them blind?

Their thoughts so centralized, their souls self – absorbed, their god's teachings all but ignored.

The divinities replaced by the masters of iniquities, who've twisted the fates of all by changing the lies they call history.

The words of the saviors and the cherished ones, now speak the blasphemy of war on their tongues.

Fighting over slave labor to put shoes on our feet, while folks in far off countries die of nothing to eat.

We sell plastic bottled water, while the Jordan runs red, motivated by thoughts of consumption racing through our head.

Not a thought is given, riding in our s.u.v. , to the reactions of our actions that don't bother you and me.

We continue to sit comfortably in our refinanced cubicals staring at brightly lit cubicals .

We need not follow these crazed hypocrites to the end of the world

We need not let them lead us to believe that the story they've contrived is real

Simply to line their pockets with the souls they steal

The perks are so damn tempting, I've got my own d.v.d., now I can veg out to all the bullshit available through my p.c.

The world could end tomorrow and we'd be none the wiser, till it becomes a movie of the week starring Paul Reiser .

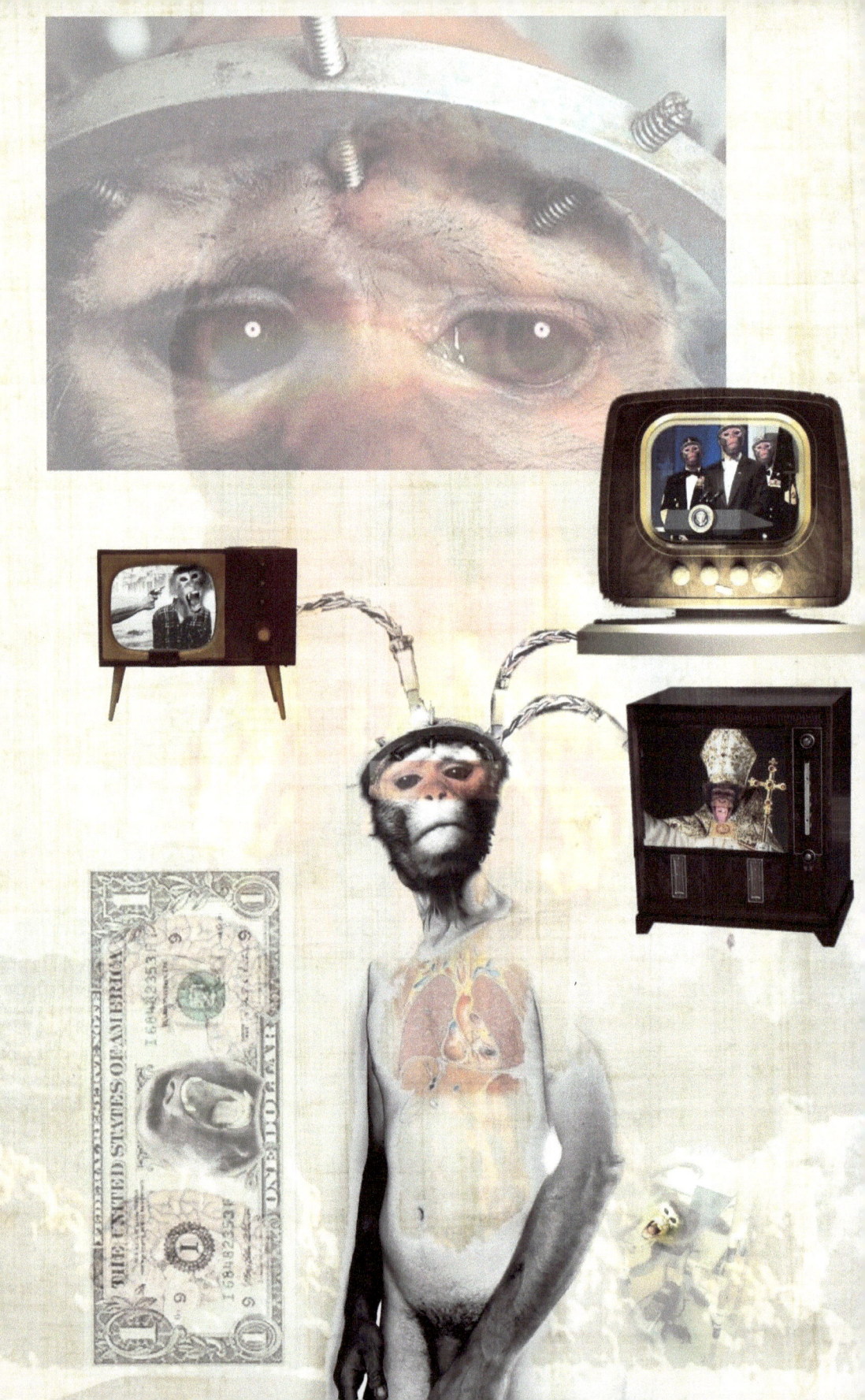

Help Us Save Tomorrow

Written: 1996

Where are we going to now?

Now that it's all gone away.

Is our love gone now?

Who will show us the way?

The darkness spreads so far

So far I can't see the end.

Where did we go wrong?

Who will save us today?

Can you show me the way?

To save today, for tomorrow

No more grief, no more sorrow

Help us save today for tomorrow

The greatest teacher we try to find, if
Buddha were yours

And Christ were mine

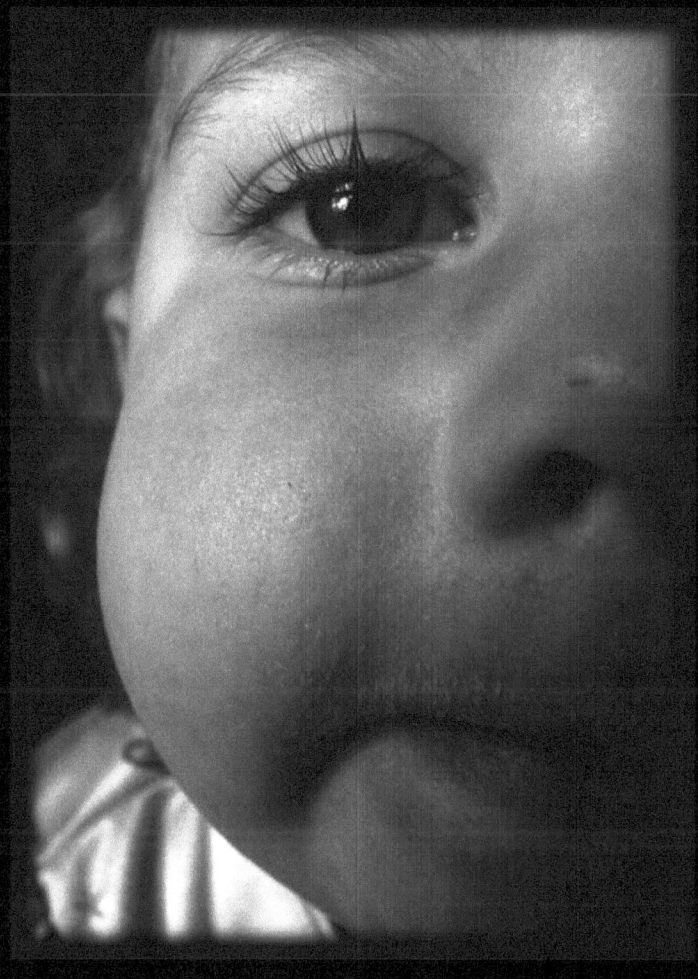

Where could we find the time to become blind

To the true salvation we would find

To help us save tomorrow

They may show you the way to save today for tomorrow

No more grief, no more sorrow, our children are the way to save today for tomorrow

Teach them well, life is hell, release them from their cell, arm them well, so they can tell us how to save
today, tomorrow.

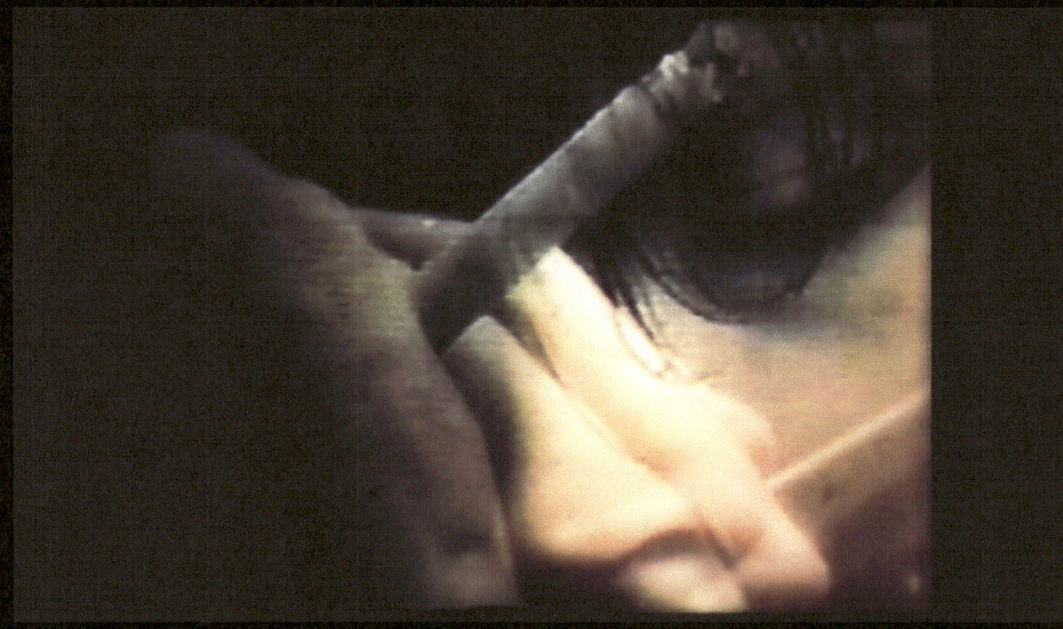

Living life between cigarettes, I sometimes wonder, what is the purpose of this 'searching for one's self' from within one's self and to whom does it benefit?

Where does it end? When do we stop fearing the love of others? When do we start loving?

When did we start fearing the love of others or the fear we have to instill in them of loving others too?

I thought I'd be growing old alone. Always thought if I made it this far, I'd be sharing love with someone.

Instead I find myself afraid . . . . afraid to love those who would love me or maybe just afraid to let them love me.

Living life between cigarettes, I find that the calluses have grown over my throbbing, aching, and empty heart.

Who 'out there' wants a broken man? Who 'out there' can share my broken dreams?

Whatever happened to the boy who ran through the wood reliving his father's war memories with a plastic gun and trusty sidekick . . . . . his dog?

Where did his dreams go? His aspiration spent .

What of the smile that parted his lips that has long passed from his memory? What of the tears he once shed in memorial for the passing of those smiles. If only to cry. Where has it all gone?

There was a time when love touched deep, when there was still a belief in love.

The last tears shed were for guilt not loss nor love.

Living life between cigarettes is slow suicide. Not unlike the suicide of letting everyone walk away with a piece of you, till there is nothing left.

But how does the cycle end, or does it? Oh, this addiction.

I keep waiting for something to change it all, trying to find the inspiration and ability to change things, but find nothing. Can nothing be done or is there nothing to do?

Can nothing change the circumstances of this existence? Will there ever be satisfaction of my craving for something more from it all?

Life is not what was expected. Guess it never is. But this one seem melancholy. I exist in grey. Never quite white, never quite black. Somewhere between leaded and unleaded, regular and sugar free, decaffeinated or fully loaded , happiness and misery, death and life, indifference.

Light another one

The shows almost over

Seeking enlightenment through death seems the religious way

I seek enlightenment through life.

I do not think this can happen whilst mucking around in the same bullshit as everybody else, but it remains a means of escaping the nullifying numbness of being.

What defines my reality? How does it relate and inter relate to your reality? What difference does it make in the "grande scheme" of existence. The overall collective social consciousness and one's spiritual development and improvement are affected how by individual exploration and discovery?

Where did you go?

Are you listening?

Got a light?

These are merely the depraved rantings of an alcoholic infused state of heightened perception of the world, myself, society, spirituality, and craving.

Living life between cigarettes I've come to realize how great an influence lust plays on the human animal.

Lust and confusion.

Living life between cigarettes, I ponder my purpose.

Living life between cigarettes, I wonder where you are.

Masters Of Iniquity part 2

Written: 2004

(they) rise up against me

Masters of iniquity

Oppressors of my soul

Reward them with evil

They are our enemies'

They work their iniquities

Everyone is filthy

The beginning of the end

Casting oppression with wrath

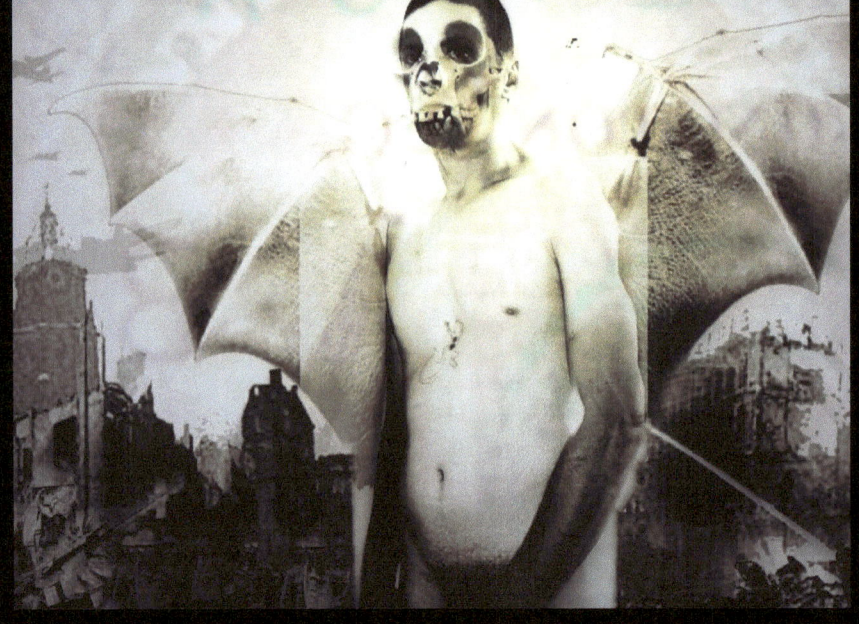

Fearful and trembling

(the) horror surrounds me

If I could leave this grim society

(leave) the masters of iniquity

Running from the storm

Divide their voices

Let them die

Send them straight to hell

His words were smooth

Smoother than butter

But war was in his heart

His words were soft

Softer than oil

Fear and horror

The beginning of the end

My heart is sore

Pains within me

They see no change

They fear no god

Make your peace with him

Listen to me

Judge me by my strengths

They are my enemies

Masters of iniquity

Oppressors of my soul

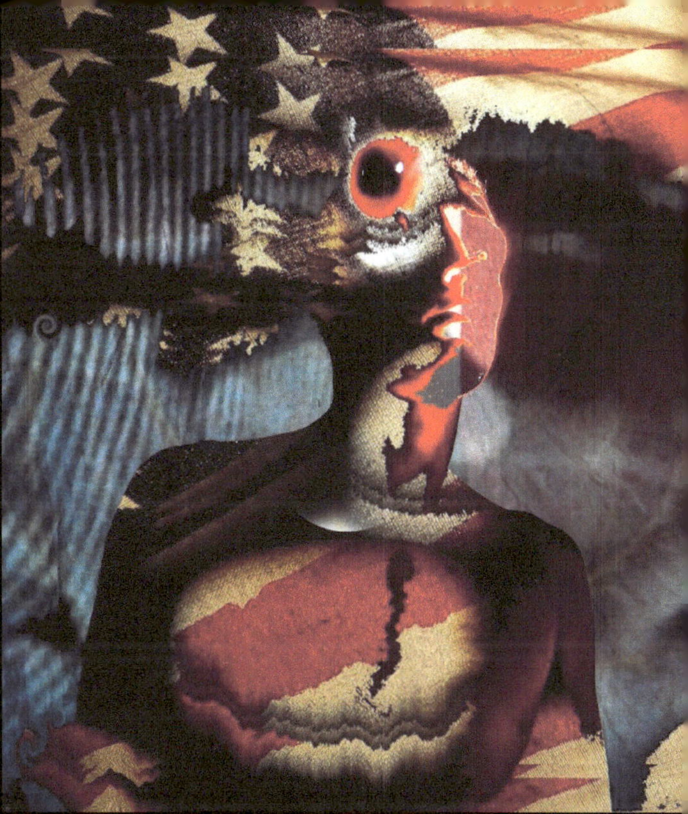

For them I do mourn

The voice of the enemy

Enemy of humanity

Masters of iniquity

Oppression in their wrath

Destroy the masters of iniquity

Destroy them in my heart, oppressors of my soul. Fly away. Hide from the storm

Red In My Eyes

Written: 1996

Walkin with my right shoe on

Chewin bitter bubble gum

Got my hat pulled low

Shades on my nose

I am a love child

Born from hate

I use my smile for bait

Come feel my charms

Cum in my arms

For an afternoon I'm great

You want my heart, your too late

Hello mary jane

Hello again

No surprise

Red in my eyes

She tells me no lies

Chucks smack the street

To a melancholy beat

Life's a bowl a cherries

Filled with nuttin but hoes

I'm a love child

Born from hate

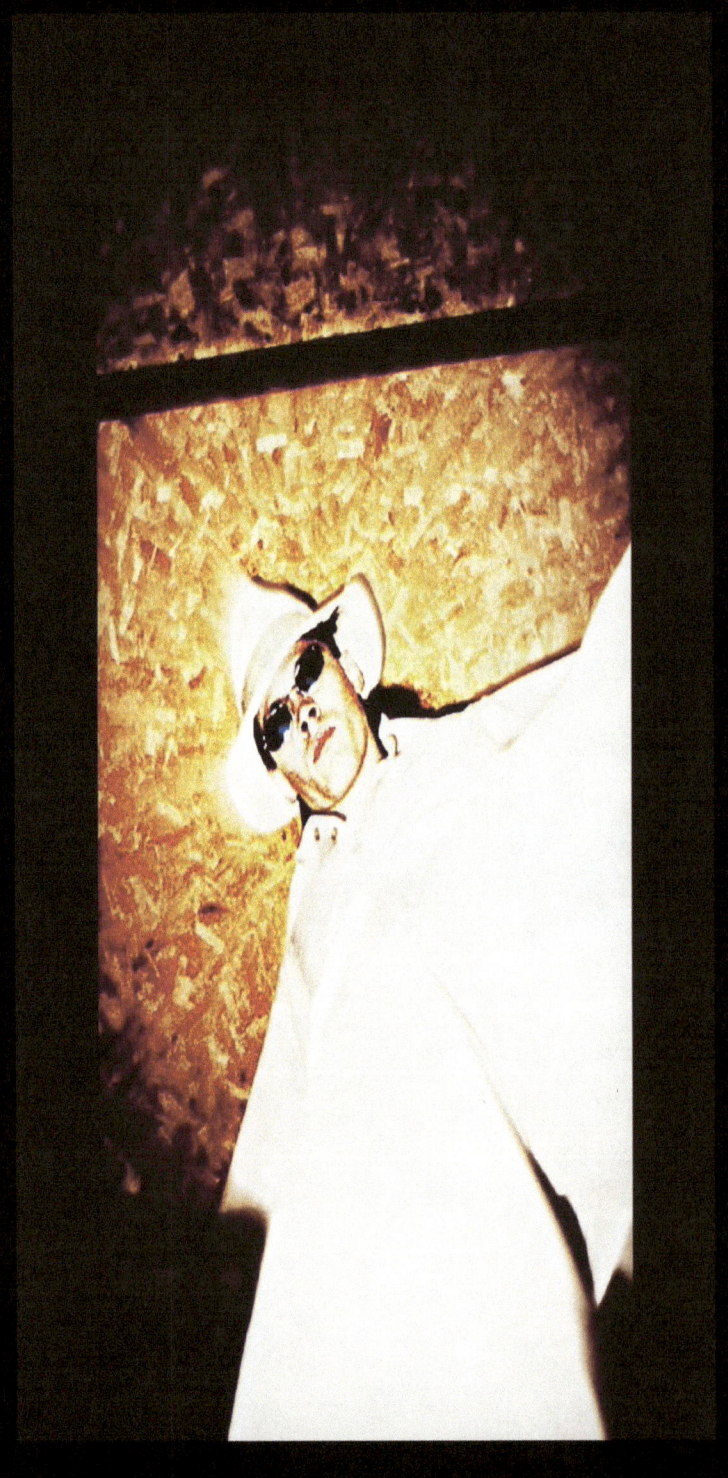

I use my smile for bait

Yellow stains on my fingers

The smell still lingers

Hello mary jane

Hello again

No surprise

Red in my eyes

She tells no lies

It's too late, I'm at your door

I need refilled, I need some more

Cotton stuffed mouth

I struggle to your house

I am self medicated

Always inebriated

Hello mary jane

Hello again

No surprise

Red in my eyes

She tells no lies

I am a love child

Born from hate

Can't be saved

It's too late

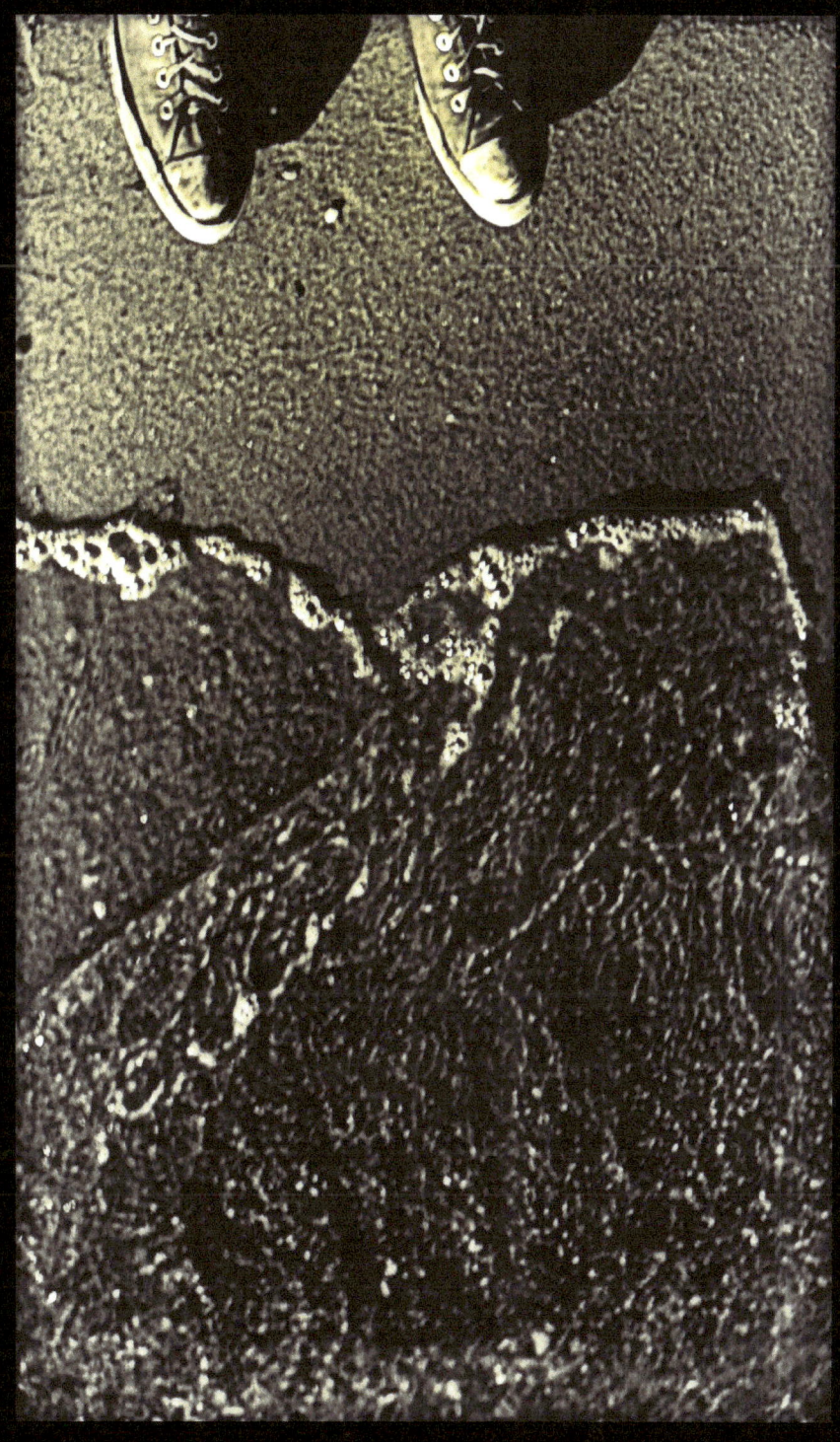

Pinocchio meets the Blue Fairy

These puppet strings have broken free

Now I'm free to follow, or run from destiny

To shape my future, and not let it shape me

Without strings to guide me what will I be

What shall I seek? What shall I see?

What strings will I find to bind the arms

That cannot move without them

Legs that cannot dance, long for strings to bind them.

The mind longs for more

Where is the puppet master?

What does he want of me, where has he gone?

Who shall give me direction?

Can I, am I, able to do this alone?

I try to lift my loosely jointed arms

I strain to lift my loosely jointed legs

To no avail

Then she lifted me up

Then I was inspired

Then Gepetto, I became a real boy!

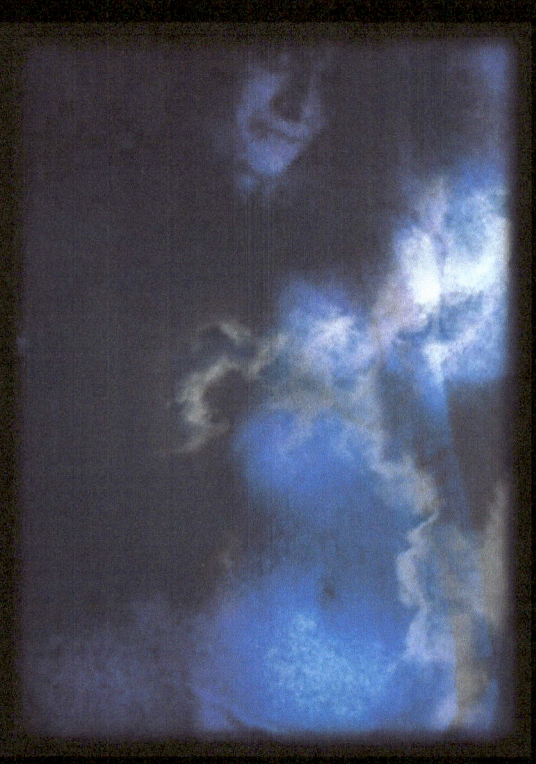

No Good

No Better

Written: 1994

So I'm no good, well your no better

I'm no good, your no better

No, I'm not great

Can not appreciate

That your no better

So you think you know the world in which you walk

Of which you talk about

What's right, what's wrong

When you've been outta touch far to long

And you think you know what's right for me

For you

You want to tell me how to live my life to be like you

And so you say:

I'm no good, well your no better

Well I know good, you know better

So I say

Wait for the day when it all comes back on you

All the judgment that you cast

While I walked on splintered glass

How you told I was a fool, tried to make me out an ass

Telling you know better than god, than man . . . . and

I'm no good, and your no better. I Know good, you know better. I'm no good, you know better. I'm no good.

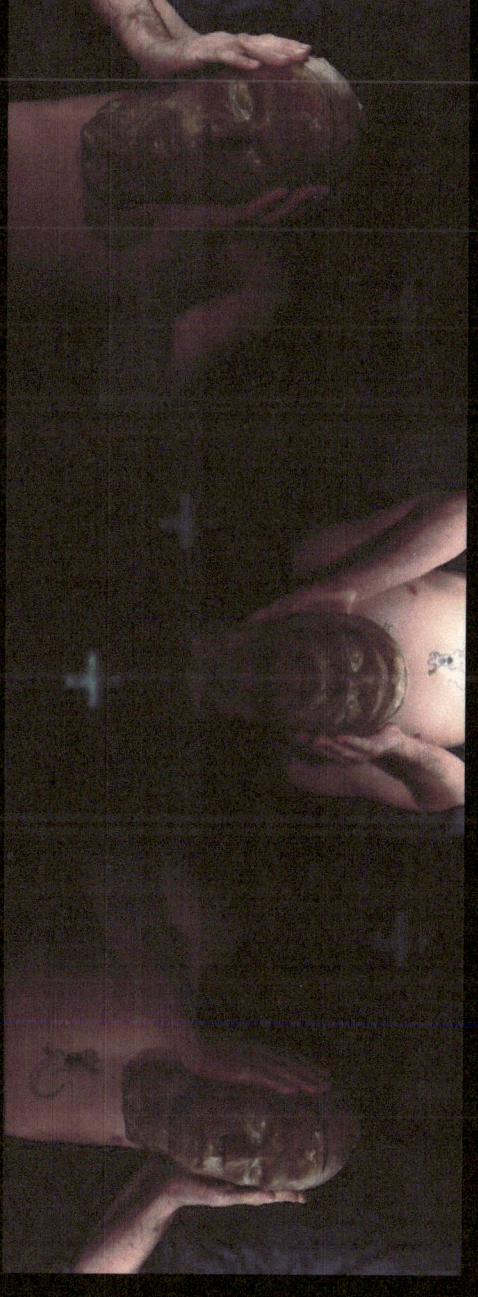

Through the tobacco smoke that hung in the air, like darkness clings to night

Sheen the brightness of her internal light

Shining from within, gleaning all about, glowing through her hazel eyes that never show signs of doubt.

Sure of who she is once more, as she stands before me, blocking the door

I cannot treat her so common, can't treat her like another one night whore.

The morning sun shone through the window behind her.

In the light she bathes where darkness cannot bind her.

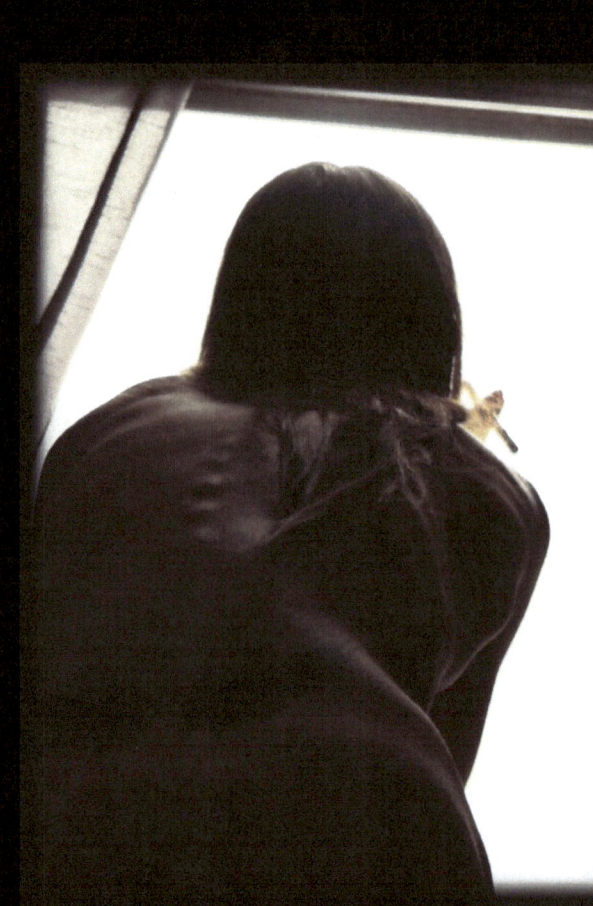

As the light fractures in Technicolor streaming, she radiates a glow all her own.

In her actions lye great meaning.

She will not let me walk away, wishing that I will let her stay.

I know she's different, though I'm not sure why.

I would like her to stay though my fears call me to run far away

Afraid of her

Afraid of me

No simpler emotions could there

What primal instincts draw her to me? What emotions await to be set free?

Far away from the dying wake of love . . . . there is left only me

To feel Nothing

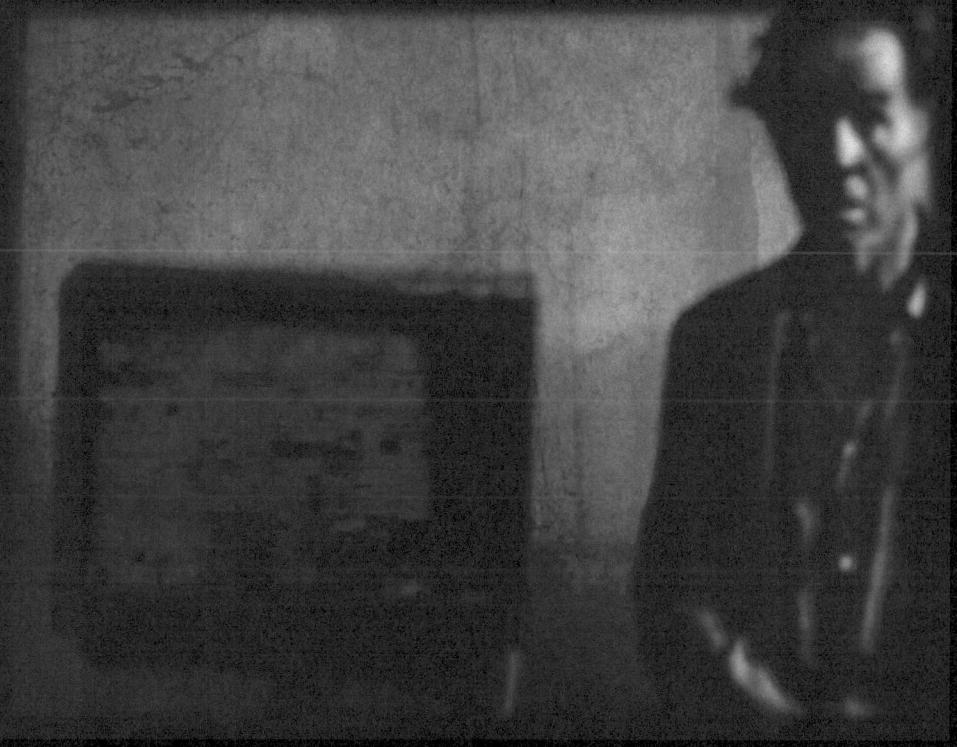

Feeling nothing has been like nothing I have ever felt

In the struggle to feel something you may loose yourself

When you feel what you thought you wanted

It turns out not to be the feeling you thought

Your left with the feeling you just felt

Abandoning the thought of which, your hand you have delt,

Causes one to grow hard and long for the feelings

You may never have felt

The Life Between Cigarettes part 2

Since your gone, I've been living life between cigarettes

They say absents makes the heart grow fonder

They say

Who are they? Did they ever meet you?

I think of my life as a million lifetimes ago, and yet it was only yesterday

I think of the lives I have surrounded, and the lives that have surrounded me

I think of those I have loved and wondered if I really ever loved at all

Living life between cigarettes I wonder if you think about me. I sometimes wonder why I think of you

I sit with Mathew Arnold on the shores of dover beach and discuss the salvation of men and their dreams

I see the seasons pass and yet I do not see you

Some have sought your place at my table , yet I tell them I'm awaiting your arrival

But I sit alone

Since your gone, my thoughts have become self-reflective, yet I continue to try to find distractions.

Has everyone . . . .everything just been a distraction from life, from the pseudo life of the mind

Can we detach the pseudo life from the physicality of living, (Or) from the emotion of having lived?

 Since your gone, I've been living life between cigarettes thinking about the girl who wouldn't let me in

I just stood in the doorway and looked at you.

Distance makes the heart grow absent.

Absence makes the heart grow fonder of what? Distance?

Am I afraid of being lonely? Am I afraid of being alone? Am I afraid?

The clock ticks away the minutes, the moon goes through phases, but what does it mean?

What does each passing minute bring? What does each passing minute take away?

Only time will tell.

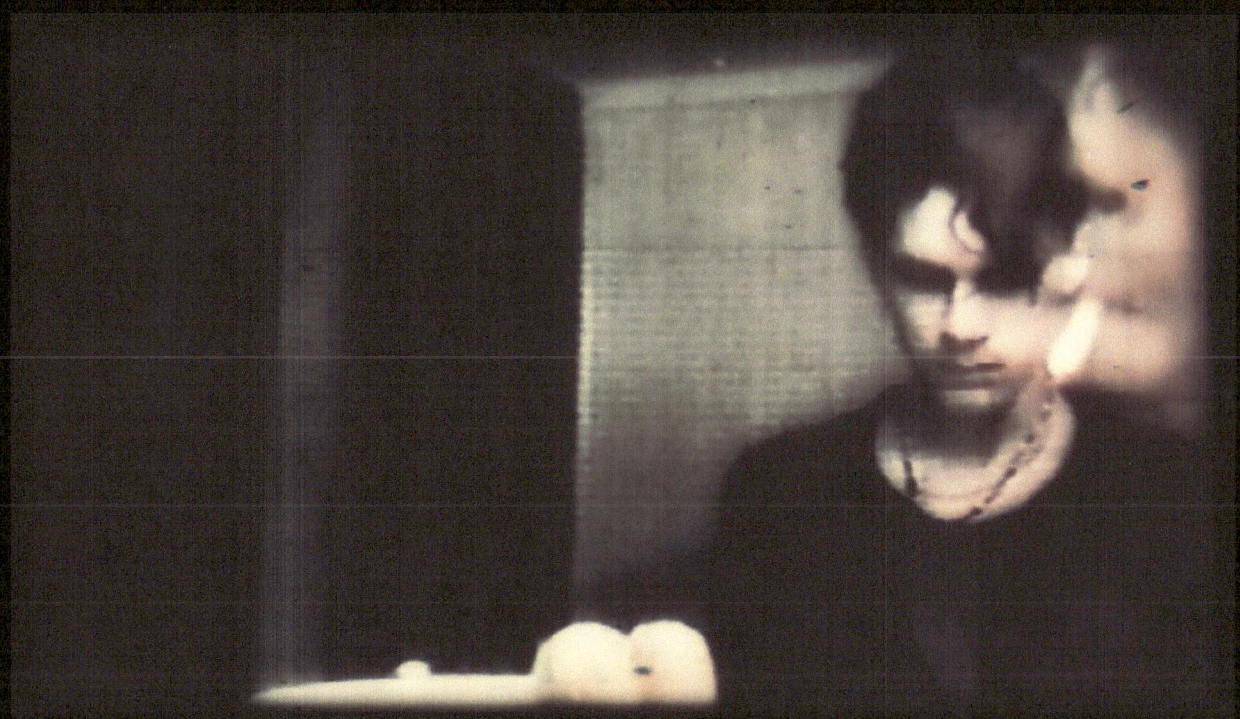

I think of those I've loved, and those who would love me.

Are you one of them?

Did I ever really love at all?

Do I know what love is?

Do you?

Would we find it together? Would we?

I think of the things we've done, and the people we knew, do they still know us?

Do we still know us?

Where are we going? Where are we now? Time only brings questions without answers.

Without answers are there questions? Can we find the answers? Do we wish too? Shall we find them together? Can the answers only be found apart?

And there ....alone.
in the darkness
alone in a crowded room
I saw you creeping
tip toeing, clawing at my door
slipping by the window
passing through the corners of my eye
I heard you calling
wanting to steal me away
haunting me, taunting me
wanting of me to stay
in the dark places
in the corners of the world
in the shadows of the mind.
hiding away your faces
in folds wich have come to bind . . . .
to the darkness that follows or to
the past I can't leave behind.

David Cartwright 1972 -
"Enter the Depression, welcome me in"

And there in the darkness I stood. With only the fear and pain to guild me
the fear . . . the fear of pain, the pain of fear
Till confusion and fustration overwhelm.
The frustration of confusion, the confusion of frustration.
all of which lead to anger and wraith and retribution
of all manner rought up my shoulders to unleash hell
unto the world around me and in the wake of my unleashed tourment
reigns chaos conjured from deep below.
only to find that my only victim is myself.
myself, my fear, my pain, my confusion, my frustration, my wraith,
my retribution, my tourment, my chaos, myself.
And no one, but I, noticed the dispair of the reality of my existence
of the existence of my reality in utter shambles.
Clean up your own mess and let me manage mine.

"dispairity"
David Cartwright
disordian failure

today

As the hours, minutes, and days pass by

I find less room for thoughts of you and i

I'm just sitting waiting to die . . . . . . as the years roll by

I'm thinking about a place far off in my inner space

It's not prettier there but I can hide from the ugliness that surrounds

From the deprivation that abounds . . . . . hiding from the fears that hound

That taunt, that flaunt deceit.

What you see is what you've done

Not sure of what you've become, where the forces that be should make us one

Stare into the gazing pool, see the reflection of the fool.

Why are we so blind to see what things could be as we desperately slide down the razors edge.

Yesterday I saw the cliffhanger at the dime store theatre show

I won't go back today

It's always more exciting when we're not sure which way the story will go.

Nothing but today and me.

Today I fear nothing but today and me.

The crickets were silent when the rain came

The thunder rolled in the distance, the lightening silhouetted the trees

The electricity charged the air, the humidity made everything sticky

Standing in the rain, my tears were hidden, though I no longer feel like crying

The beer was warm and stale, the cigarettes were damp.

Lightening flashed across the sky, I had come here to drink and die

But without rhyme nor reason why, life went on and so did i.

But where is he now , that guy. If he could see me now he'd say I'm living a lie.

I've sold out and lost touch. I don't think that I miss him very much.

But if I feel for a moment what was real

would it be him I'm trying to conceal

what about the guy I saw yesterday?

Is he the one who got in my way?

I can only live with who is here today

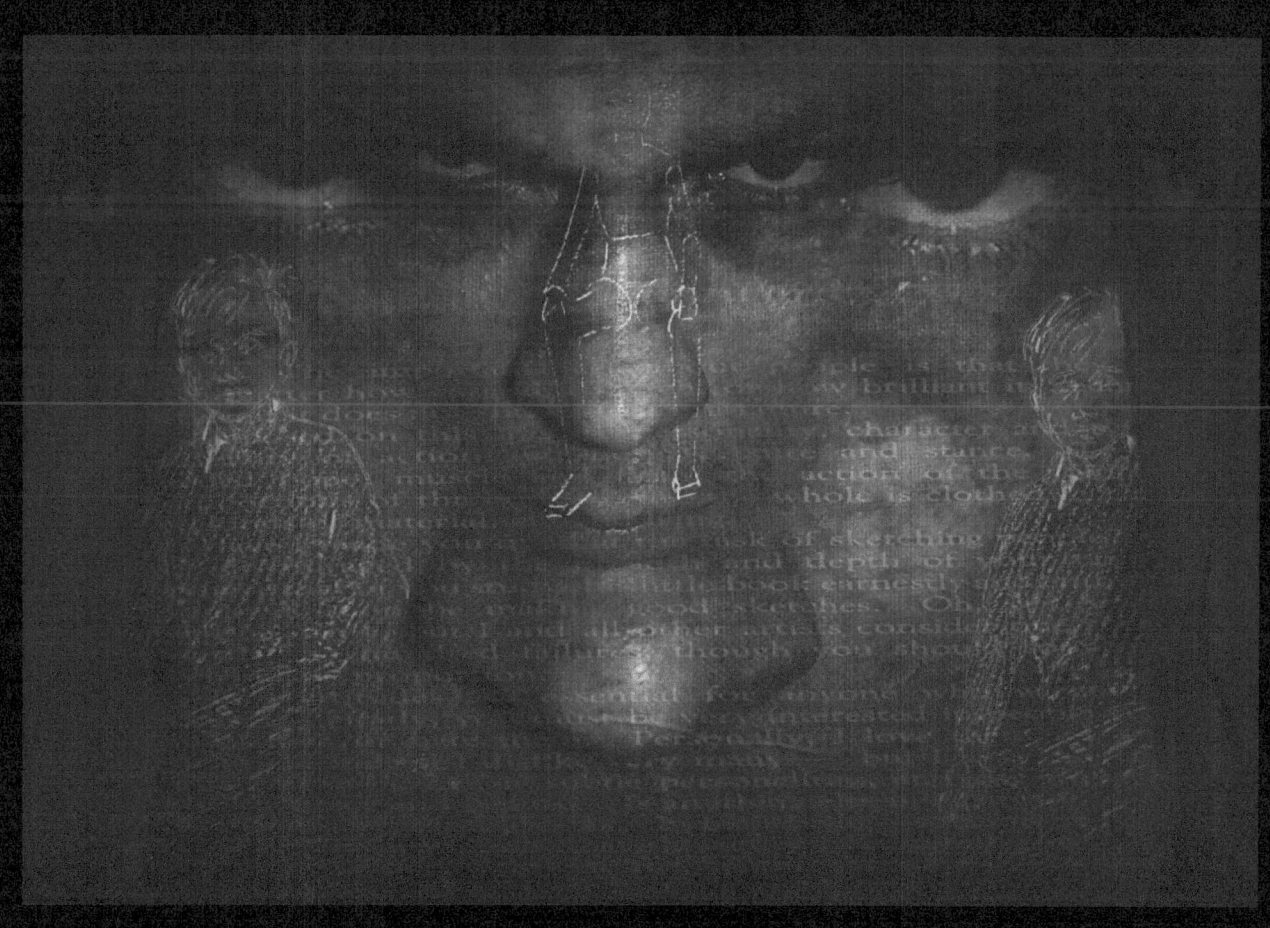

The author/photographer : David Cartwright

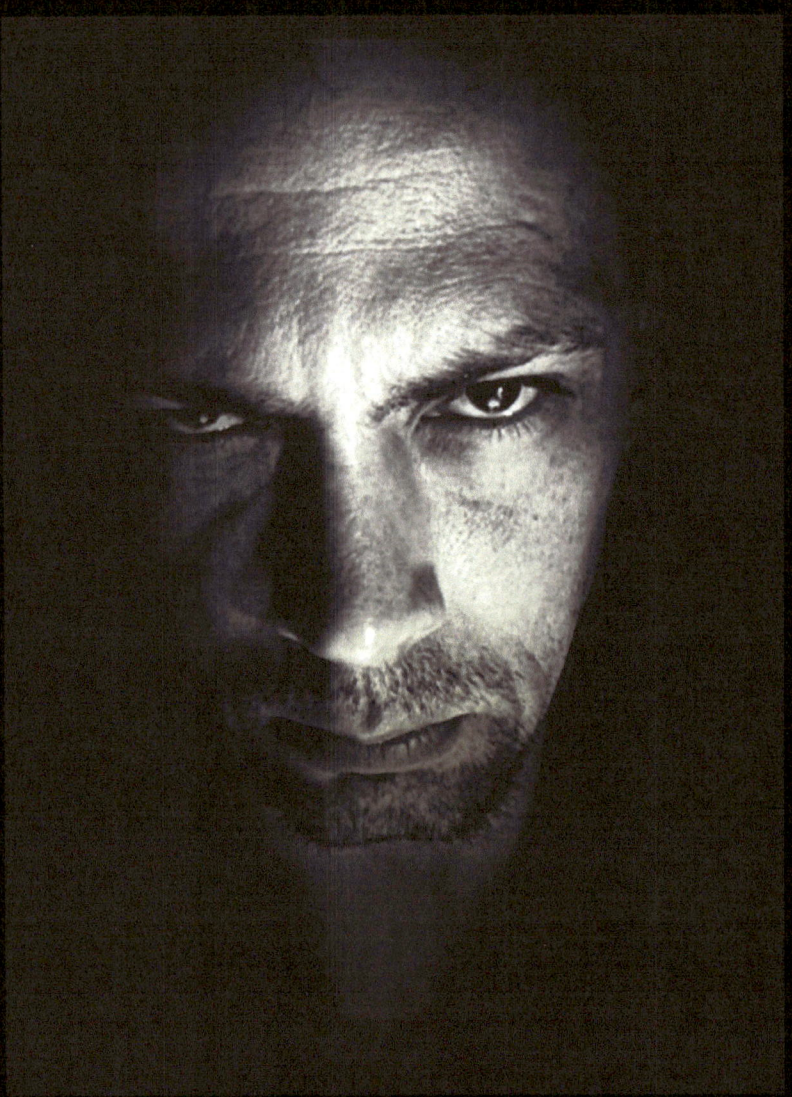

http://www.flickr.com/photos/bobthebuilderoflove/

bobthebuilderoflove.deviantart.com/

www.youtube.com/user/bobthebuilderoflove

www.saatchionline.com/bobzstudiooffoto

www.modelmayhem.com/bobthebuilderoflove

www.riseart.com/user/bobstudiofoto

www.ingramcontent.com/pod-product-compliance
Lightning Source LLC
Chambersburg PA
CBHW050911180526
45159CB00007B/2870